"Jerome Rothenberg is one of the truly contemporary American poets who has returned U.S. poetry to the mainstream of international modern literature. At the same time he is a true autochthon. Only here and now could have produced him – a swinging orgy of Martin Buber, Marcel Duchamp, Gertrude Stein, and Sitting Bull. No one writing poetry today has dug deeper into the roots of poetry."

– Kenneth Rexroth

"The significance of Jerome Rothenberg's animating spirit looms larger every year. [He] is the ultimate 'hyphenated' poet: critic-anthropologist-editor-anthologist-performer-teacher-translator, to each of which he brings an unbridled exuberance and an innovator's insistence on transforming a given state of affairs."

– Charles Bernstein

"Jerome Rothenberg is a DNA spaceman exploring the mammal caves of Now."

– Michael McClure

# GEMATRIA COMPLETE

## JEROME ROTHENBERG

MARICK
PRESS

Library of Congress Cataloguing in Publication Data

Jerome Rothenberg
Gematria Complete

ISBN 10: 1-934851-086
ISBN 13: 978-1-934851-081

Copyright © by Jerome Rothenberg, 2009
Edited by Ilya Kaminsky
Design and typesetting by Sean Tai
Cover design by Sean Tai

Printed and bound in the United States

Marick Press
P.O. Box 36253
Grosse Pointe Farms
Michigan 48236
www.marickpress.com

Mariela Griffor, Publisher

Distributed by
Small Press Distribution
and
Wayne State University Press

*For Edmond Jabès, in memory*

The desert
speaks.

ACKNOWLEDGMENTS

The predecessor to this volume was published as *Gematria* by Sun & Moon Press, Los Angeles, in 1994, and the sequence "14 Stations" appeared earlier in Jerome Rothenberg's *Seedings & Other Poems* (New Directions, 1996) and *Writing Through: Translations & Variations* (Wesleyan University Press, 2004). *Delight/Délices & Other Gematria*, with drawings by Ian Tyson and French translations by Nicole Peyrafitte, was published by Editions Ottezec, Nimes, in 1998, and several broadsides in collaboration with Ian Tyson have appeared over the years. *All rights have since devolved to the author, but gratitude for publication is strong and ongoing.*

CONTENTS

A Gematria for Jackson Mac Low                                  1
3 Gematrias for John Cage                                       1
Language Gematria for Charles Bernstein                         2
3 Gematrias for Armand Schwerner                                3
2 Gematrias for Howard Norman                                   3
"Seventy": A Birthday Gematria for Allan Kaprow                 4
Three Gematrias for Tom Phillips                                5
A Gematria for Lynn Luria-Sukenick                              7
Tens, for David Meltzer                                         8

25 GEMATRIA                                                     9

GEMATRIAS 12 × 22                                              13
First Gematria                                                 15
Second Gematria                                                20
Third Gematria                                                 26
Fourth Gematria                                                32
Fifth Gematria                                                 38
Sixth Gematria                                                 43
Seventh Gematria                                               49
Eighth Gematria                                                55
Ninth Gematria                                                 61
Tenth Gematria                                                 67
Eleventh Gematria                                              73
Twelfth Gematria                                               79

| | |
|---|---|
| MORE GEMATRIAS (1-100) | 87 |
| | |
| BEYOND GEMATRIA | 127 |
| Gematria One | 129 |
| Gematria Two | 129 |
| Gematria Three | 130 |
| Gematria Four | 131 |
| Gematria Five | 131 |
| Gematria Six | 132 |
| Gematria Seven | 133 |
| Domestic Gematria | 133 |
| A Gematria for Horsemen | 134 |
| Khurbn Gematria | 135 |
| Paper Airs | 137 |
| Cold Rivets | 139 |
| | |
| 14 STATIONS | 145 |
| The First Station: Auschwitz-Birkenau | 147 |
| The Second Station: Babi Yar | 148 |
| The Third Station: Buchenwald | 149 |
| The Fourth Station: Belzec | 149 |
| The Fifth Station: Bergen-Belsen | 150 |
| The Sixth Station: Gross-Rosen | 151 |
| The Seventh Station: Dachau | 151 |
| The Eighth Station: Chelmno | 152 |
| The Ninth Station: Treblinka | 153 |
| The Tenth Station: Mauthausen | 154 |
| The Eleventh Station: Maidanek | 155 |
| The Twelfth Station: Sobibor | 156 |
| The Thirteenth Station: Ravensbruck | 157 |
| The Fourteenth Station: Stutthof | 158 |
| | |
| POST/FACE | 159 |

# GEMATRIA
# COMPLETE

## A GEMATRIA FOR JACKSON MAC LOW

CHANCE

made it happen.

---

Chance = 310.

## 3 GEMATRIAS FOR JOHN CAGE

ROARATORIO (1)

A new
place.

ROARATORIO (2)

The leeks
& the fire.

ROARATORIO (3)

The magicians
return.

---

Roaratorio = 625.

## A LANGUAGE GEMATRIA FOR CHARLES BERNSTEIN

Divination.

Like the bed
in the firmament.

•

Language.

Our voice.
& your eye.

Colors
limped.

•

The thick darkness
shall rule you.

Language
shall rule you.

## 3 GEMATRIAS FOR ARMAND SCHWERNER

### THE TABLETS (1)

Fearing
to give light.

### THE TABLETS (2)

The moon
will choose.

### THE TABLETS (3)

Sheol
in Sodom

---

The Tablets = 443.

## 2 GEMATRIAS FOR HOWARD NORMAN

### WILDERNESS (1)

They emptied it out.

### WILDERNESS (2)

Your eyes
in the tree.

---

Wilderness = 400.

## "SEVENTY": A BIRTHDAY GEMATRIA FOR ALLAN KAPROW

so
I bring him
the wine

& stretch out
in life
howling

like the sand
in my ears

these were
    poor
were worn old
    & were sore

his life
    in your hand
[or] in our hand

trembling
in greatness

so
right
correct

whatsoever

*Paris 1997*

## THREE GEMATRIAS FOR TOM PHILLIPS

[1] Tom = 9 + 1 + 40 = 50

all
the man

his blood
red

a sea
to his hand

in the night


[2] Phillips = 80 + 10 + 30 + 10 + 80 + 60 = 270

evil
displeases

anger
cries out

a stranger
descending

was angry
& hurt

"foreigner
"alien

"tender
"like lambs

[3] Humument = 5 + 6 + 40 + 6 + 40 + 70 + 50 + 9 = 226

you have spoken

according to
its length

spread abroad
& to the side

before our eyes

like so

## A GEMATRIA FOR LYNN LURIA-SUKENICK
*in memoriam*

to give light
(she said)

& to be lifted up
according to your word

appearances
will fly

the cricket
speaking

blameless
in the sand

your eyes
will praise

will look upon
the wilderness

*& in the lion's name
will make it shine*

## TENS, FOR DAVID MELTZER

Ten riches.

Ten fountains.

Ten wrestlings.

Ten cities.

Ten wonders.

Ten hairs.

Ten
& ten.

# 25 GEMATRIA

*Translated & composed from traditional
Hebrew sources with Harris Lenowitz*

LIGHT
A mystery.

                        EYE
                        Silver.

THE UPPER WORLD
Is all the chariot.

HE & HE
This & this.

                        METATRON
                        The beard.
                        The beard.

MESSENGER
Five.

THE WITNESS
A jewel.

                        THE BODY
                        The reward.

THE WORLD/THE YEAR/THE SOUL
Evening.
Morning.
Noon.

FIRST ADAM
Hell is open.

                        MOSES
                        I am.
                        I am.
                        I am.

THE GARDEN
Shadow.
Stone.
The Brain.

THE SOUL OF ADAM
Lilith.

                        ISRAEL
                        El Song.

REBEKKA
This.
12.

THE RIVER
The prayerbook.

INCENSE
The ark.
613.

WISDOM
Is.
Was.
Will be.

MESSIAH
Snake.

THE DEVIL
Fat-ash.

THIS POPE
This garbage.

DOMINUS
Demonus.

MONEY
The tree.

*& the king said
to Haman: the money
will be yours*

DEATH
903.

ISRAEL ALONE
Therefore.

# GEMATRIAS
## 12 X 22

## FIRST GEMATRIA

ENOUGH

or too much.

---

THE BAT

His yellow
angel.

---

THE BORDER (1)

A hundred.

THE BORDER (2)

Alone.

---

EYES

A hole
& an amethyst.

---

### EVENING

Evil.

---

### A FLAG

Living, raw
garments of.

---

### IN THE GARDEN

In the sea.

---

### Our Dreams

sprouting
forth.

---

### God (1)

A flame.

### God (2)

A terror.

A HOOK

One part
linen.

---

THE MAIDEN (1)

Stretched out
& ready.

THE MAIDEN (2)

Compasses
night.

---

TO THE MOON (1)

The shore
a small matter.

TO THE MOON (2)

Witnesses
below.

---

THE NEEDY

shall judge.

---

IN THE SADDLE

Red, ruddy
nuts.

---

SALT (1)

A flood.

SALT (2)

Like the stars.

SALT (3)

Dreaming.

---

GEMATRIA 428

I have sinned
into freedom.

---

IN SODOM (1)

A garden.
A wall.

IN SODOM (2)

At what time
shall we come?

---

THESE

Those.

---

IN THE [AMERICAN] TREE
*for Ron Silliman*

(1)
Dark.
Damsel.
Dan.

(2)
The glorious
anger.

———————

WAILING

A brick
in my mouth.

———————

WITH US

Against us.

## SECOND GEMATRIA
"Together"

### TOGETHER

A feast
when he came.

---

### IN THE SHADOW (1)

I am
your mother.

### IN THE SHADOW (2)

A stolen
womb.

---

### THE IDOLS (1)

The garden
is hot.

### THE IDOLS (2)

who fed you.

---

### MY MOUTH

A hole.

---

LICE (1)

Like fat
from her issue.

LICE (2)

Hollow
& dark.

---

FOUR

a power
at night

fierce &
full.

---

GEMATRIA 252

Horses
in Eden.

---

IN A VISION (1)

A harlot.

IN A VISION (2)

His glory
perhaps.

---

AN ANGEL (1)

The cup,
the little owl.

AN ANGEL (2)

By himself.

AN ANGEL (3)

Amen.

---

AS YOU ARE

A child
& a poor man.

---

DEATH (1)

The yellow
angels
of God.

DEATH (2)

The moon
like a stranger.

---

DEW

A rebuke.

---

EASTWARD (1)

The mountains.

EASTWARD (2)

A ladder
& flaming.

---

YOUR FACE

I will know
in a dream.

---

GEMATRIA 123

A womb
in a vision.


The thief
& the beast.

---

IN MY MOUTH

Red
terror.

---

### THEIR LIVES (1)

like a garden.

### THEIR LIVES (2)

like a stone.

---

### GEMATRIA 20

The falcon.

The hooks.

His hands
will swoop down.

---

### A WOMB (1)

Bruised
& sore.

### A WOMB (2)

God
was slain.

---

### SHE SAID:

Bruised
testicles.

---

A FACE (1)

My mouth
knew him.

A FACE (2)

I redeem
from the sea.

A FACE (3)

kept murmuring.

---

A MAN WHO SEES

Knowing
a window.

## THIRD GEMATRIA
"Lot in Sodom"

**THE ADULTERER**

He found her.

---

**I COMMAND YOU:**

Eat!

---

**FOR A HARLOT (1)**

She gave birth
& he rolled.

**FOR A HARLOT (2)**

Her blood
a measure.

---

**THE STONE**

crushed
her hands.

---

A FINGER (1)

Through his ear,
into her mouth.

A FINGER (2)

To swell
her belly.

---

A BREAST

I will come
in her hand.

---

IN A DREAM (1)

To pronounce it unclean.

IN A DREAM (2)

Sweet unto me, dear.

IN A DREAM (3)

It shall be circumcised.

---

THE SINNERS

mingled.

---

### SODOM (1)

Lewdness
shall cease.

### SODOM (2)

Lewdness,
I pray thee.

### SODOM (3)

Lewdness—
what is it?

---

### HIS FORESKIN

& a knob.

---

### AS HE WRESTLED

The stone
became hot.

---

### HER BELLY (1)

Her strength
when I come.

### HER BELLY (2)

& the wheat
at the entrance.

THE TOUCHER

& the one who touches.

---

TO ONAN (1)

Two days—
then he hardened.

TO ONAN (2)

In their mouths.

---

IN THE RAIN

Streaked
dainties.

---

THEIR PORTION (1)

The dream
will perish.

THEIR PORTION (2)

They shall touch
his tail.

---

A SPIRIT (1)

Rings.
A dark
stone.

A SPIRIT (2)

Onan
commanded him.

## HIS VOICE

Alive
in her womb.

---

## PORNOGRAPHIC POEM (1)

A breast
will be glorified

## PORNOGRAPHIC POEM (2)

Goats
will be slain.

## PORNOGRAPHIC POEM (3)

What is it?
What is it?

---

## IN THE MORNING (1)

Full
heavy
testicles.

## IN THE MORNING (2)

A bird
in your hand.

**THE BEARD**
  *for Michael McClure*

To eat from
your belly.

———————————

**A BLOSSOM**

Her beautiful
mouth.

## FOURTH GEMATRIA
"In the Shadow"

### WITHOUT GOD

Without terror.

---

### GEMATRIA 372

Seven.
Plenty.
A week.

---

### MY HEART (1)

Flaming.

### MY HEART (2)

Blood.

---

### THE SIGN

I see
a word / spoken.

---

IN THE SHADOW (1)

A womb
he devours.

IN THE SHADOW (2)

I am
nothing.

---

TESTIMONY
    *for Charles Reznikoff*

The light.
The terror.

---

BURNING

Your beautiful
mind.

Dead
at the entry.

---

A FOUNTAIN (1)

An eye.

A FOUNTAIN (2)

Shall I hide?

## A WINDOW

Wherein
& forward.

---

## COLORS (1)

Yellow
stars.

## COLORS (2)

His red
throne.

---

## THE CANDLESTICK / THE FIRE

The yellow
Baal
eats
like a god.

---

## A VISION (1)

Beat it
with power.

## A VISION (2)

God
is crushed.

---

## YOU

& a double.

---

THE CITY

Broken.

•

Void.

---

FLESH (1)

An ark
& a worm.

FLESH (2)

Before
& bitter.

---

THE ROCK

fell.

---

A CURSE

Your father
shall live.

―――――――――

A CLOUD (1)

In wood.

―――――――――

ALL

or enough.

―――――――――

CITIES, CITIES

Silver
& speckled.

A tree
fallen down.

―――――――――

My country
a fire.

•

Divided.

―――――――――

A CLOUD (2)

Forever.

| THE VOICE (1) | THE VOICE (2) |
|---|---|
| will answer. | A voice. |

# FIFTH GEMATRIA
"Among"

**AMONG (1)**

spiritum
descended.

**AMONG (2)**

Breath
trickled down.

———————

**YOUR SHOES**

& the wind.

———————

**A DOOR (1)**

White.

**A DOOR (2)**

Open.

———————

**LOUDLY**

A bell.

———————

They stripped
& let her be.

They stripped
& she came.

———————

ROOMS

Those that were numbered.

———————

PASSOVER

passed.

———————

NIGHT (1)

The melons.

NIGHT (2)

& they rolled.

———————

THE LIGHT

Like God
in Sodom.

———————

## AN INHERITANCE

Shut—
like the rain.

---

## UNDER HIM

Houses of
lusting.

•

United
delight.

---

## GEMATRIA 316

The man
was aroused.

The rod
heated up.

---

## GOING / NUTS

You eat
your face.

---

THE SHOVELS

Dyed red.

---

AGAINST YOU

Your anger.
Your anger.

---

"AND FRAIL WITH LONGING"

As she spoke
I dug it.

---

THE EGGS (1)   THE EGGS (2)

We came out.   On a stalk.

---

YOUR SHOES

went walking.

---

**THE EARLY RAIN**

& the wood.

---

**THE LIGHTS**

Spies
all over.

---

**WORDS**
      *for William Carlos Williams*

A red wheel
barrow.

---

Your wives
like wives.

•

Birds
in his house.

## SIXTH GEMATRIA
"Gematria"

### GEMATRIA (1)

To spy out.

### GEMATRIA (2)

I will bless them.

### GEMATRIA (3)

Shut.

G

---

### ABEL & GOD (1)

A large
banner.

### ABEL & GOD (2)

We have sinned.

E

---

### THE CAMEL

Father,
come.

M

---

### LIFE (1)

Upward
& after.

### LIFE (2)

The sword
in its place.

A

**WHITE (1)**

A wild ox
will tell them.

**WHITE (2)**

Among you.

    T

**WHITE (3)**

When they die.

---

**THE LORD (1)**

will become.

**THE LORD (2)**    R

& be.

---

**MANKIND**

Exceedingly.

    I

---

**MASTERY (1)**

Half of
my arrows.

**MASTERY (2)**    A

Violence
shall cease.

**MASTERY (3)**

The stones
blot me out.

JEALOUS

A very small                                              G
god.

---

KINDLED (1)                    KINDLED (2)

Her blood                      Thou lovest
became heated.                 Goyim.

KINDLED (3)
                                                          E
The bed
is hot.

---

LAUGHTER (1)                   LAUGHTER (2)
                                                          M
Their blood                    The window
into his nostrils.             numbed.

---

MY FATHER

One.                                                      A

---

**LIGHT (1)**

A stranger.

**LIGHT (2)**

I will see.

      **LIGHT (3)**                        T

      is great.

---

**A FLAME (1)**

Terror.

**A FLAME (2)**

                      R

One
father
which is coming.

---

**HIS GOD (1)**
A dog.

**HIS GOD (2)**     I
A beast.

      **HIS GOD (3)**

      What is it?

---

**FOR THE HOLY:**

An increase
of wonder.                             A

THE SONG (1)

The river
will change

THE SONG (2)

G

A scream
growing larger.

TERROR (1)

A flame.

TERROR (2)

E

The hands of
a grasshopper.

TERROR (3)

A sacrifice
when you came in.

TURTLE-DOVES

Lamps.

M

WE HAVE COME THROUGH!
    *for D.H. Lawrence*

From Eden.
From his bosom.

A

---

YOUR FATHER (1)

Bore the loss of it.

YOUR FATHER (2)
                T

In pain.

---

FOR A WITNESS (1)

Heat
in the garden.

FOR A WITNESS (2)
                R

Unclean
to your mind.

## SEVENTH GEMATRIA
"Dreamers"

A DREAM (1)

It had ceased
in them.

A DREAM (2)

My great
heart.

A DREAM (3)

Without
God.

---

NAKED

branches of
silver.

---

THE BEARD (1)

Before you.

THE BEARD (2)

In the tree.

---

TO ONE MADE SICK

in a dream.

―――――――――――――

THE RAVEN (1)

At evening.

THE RAVEN (2)

His voice
emptied out.

THE RAVEN (3)

Double
its color.

―――――――――――――

A FINGER

only
by its tail.

―――――――――――――

THE BREASTS

Inflamed
& scabby.

―――――――――――――

IN RIDDLES (1)

His word
has multiplied

IN RIDDLES (2)

His word
is strange.

## GEMATRIA 309

A field
within her.

•

The stars,
a calf,
& an earring.

## TESTICLES

like fire.

## THE MOON (1)

We dreamed
our bread

## THE MOON (2)

Who touches
the toucher.

Their genitals
stiffen.

•

The teeth
hard & cruel.

---

YESTERDAY (1)

The service.

YESTERDAY (2)

Her foot
between his knees.

---

THE YOUNG MEN

The birds.

---

AN EMPTY TOOTH

Dust
shining.

---

STARS

In his mouth.

---

SODOM (1)

A resting place.

SODOM (2)

Your blood.

SODOM (3)

According to his dream.

---

WE SHALL EAT

We ate.

---

AN EYE

Violets.
Jasmine.

---

**HORSES**

& a cloud.

---

**A MOTHER (1)**

Eve, or
the Falcon.

**A MOTHER (2)**

A tree which bears
no fruit.

---

**WE DREAMED**

& he changed.

# EIGHTH GEMATRIA
"Things"

WOOD (1)

Heaped up.

WOOD (2)

He has chosen.

———————

SCARLET

Except for
the bottle.

———————

QUICK FLESH

High places.

———————

THE FIRST

Rings
shall hang.

•

Double
rings.

---

A DIVORCE

Hats
& gashes.

---

SETTINGS

The woman.
The eggs.
An old father.

---

SECRETLY

Ships.

•

You shall steal.

---

GEMATRIA 162

In the tree.
In the rock.

In the image.
In the money.

## ROUNDABOUT KNOWLEDGE

A frying pan.

---

The bells
from the river.

•

A light
from the east.

---

## GEMATRIA 1030

Three
for six.

---

## WIDOWS

& hats.

---

### LIKE A DEAD MAN

Your tool
will enlarge.

---

### CHANGES (1)

A face.
A wheel.
A ladder.
A bone.

### CHANGES (2)

You will make it profane.

---

dust, earth

•

onyx / empty

---

### GEMATRIA 618

A field
& its flowers.

•

The fat ones.

**HOUSES**

Within.

---

**GEMATRIA 643**

In the visions.
In the mirrors.

---

**TWIN GEMATRIA**

(1)
Eight
with trumpets.

(2)
Trumpets
& eight.

---

## GEMATRIA 750

Two
thoughts.

Two
horns.

A year
from the city.

---

## THE END (1)

The fair
days.

## THE END (2)

The beautiful
waters.

## THE END (3)

Her sweet
mouth.

---

## GREENLY

Sarah
shot forth.

## NINTH GEMATRIA
"God"

GOD

is not.

———————————

IN THE VALLEY (1)

High.

IN THE VALLEY (2)

Look!

———————————

GEMATRIA 20

The falcon.
The hooks.

•

His hands
will swoop down.

———————————

HIS SIN (1)

The beloved.

HIS SIN (2)

He loves
a fish.

---

**YOUR FATHER**

Your enemy.

---

**GOD (1)**

A flame.

**GOD (2)**

A terror.

---

**A BOY CHILD**

His father
will gore.

---

**SACRIFICE (1)**

A goat.

**SACRIFICE (2)**

The fish.

**SACRIFICE (3)**

Alas.

---

THE FAT

& the poor.

---

His glory
weeping?

•

His robes.

---

THE BEAST (1)

An altar.

THE BEAST (2)

On a pole.

THE BEAST (3)

Devoured.

---

THE HANGED MAN

will die.

---

THE PROPHET (1)

shall lead.

THE PROPHET (2)

& the sand lizard.

THE PROPHET (3)

Someone
slain.

---

MORE

Your feet
on the earth.

---

GEMATRIA 77


Your corn.
Your mercy.

Your mercy.
Your altar.

---

MY WRATH

& an emerald.

---

A PRIEST (1)

Against her children.

A PRIEST (2)

But the hands.

---

THE NURSING FATHER

Indeed.

---

THE WATER (1)

Waters.

THE WATER (2)

Seas.

---

YOUR KIND

begot all.

---

## GEMATRIA 106

Your servants.
Your god.

Your god.
His hand.

---

### AN OFFERING (1)

I will eat
your heart.

### AN OFFERING (2)

A raw
dog.

## TENTH GEMATRIA
"Nations"

### THE GOYIM (1)

like the sand.

### THE GOYIM (2)

Their brothers.

### THE GOYIM (3)

We are undone.

---

### GEMATRIA 112

To make bricks
of the people.

To make bricks.
in your mouth.

---

### THE PEOPLE

The lice.

---

### CIRCUMCISED (1)

A blemish.

### CIRCUMCISED (2)

Is it too hard?

**THE PRIESTS**

Because of
a plague.

---

**SINAI (1)**

A ladder.

**SINAI (2)**

Perhaps.

---

**GEMATRIA 132**

To our god
from his servants.

To Baal
to our god.

---

**FOR A SIGN (1)**

A fountain.

**FOR A SIGN (2)**

Wine &
pitch.

---

**MINE EYES**

Mine affliction

## ANGELS (1)

Messengers.

## ANGELS (2)

Again.

## GEMATRIA 142

In the basin.
In my eyes.

In my eyes.
In your bowels.

## TO MY VOICE

Dumb
with sorrow.

## GEMATRIA 146

His face.
My voice.

My voice.
His eyes.

### THE OLD MAN (1)

A throne
to divide.

### THE OLD MAN (2)

& night
like the day.

---

### OVER THE BIRDS

A white
tower.

---

### BECAUSE (1)

God is
a blemish.

### BECAUSE (2)

Her nose
shall be circumcised.

### BECAUSE (3)

A baker
did bake.

---

### HE FLASHED LIGHT

with his finger.

---

## GEMATRIA 206

A word
spoken.

A pestilence.

A thing.

---

## A SHEKEL

A soul.

---

## THEIR MONEY (1)

Shining.

## THEIR MONEY (2)

A waste.

---

## GEMATRIA 303

His neck.
Your arm.

His treasure.
Your feet.

---

A NUMBER (1)

Nothing
but god.

A NUMBER (2)

Our oppression.

## ELEVENTH GEMATRIA
"Wilderness"

**WHEN HE DIED:**

My spirit was angry.

---

**HIS SPIRIT (1)**

He lighted
a pole.

**HIS SPIRIT (2)**

Like a mouth
on my hand.

---

**NORTHWARD**

& afterward.

---

**A WOUND (1)**

A pillar
& arrows.

**A WOUND (2)**

My thigh.

---

Like iron
& slime.

---

### WORDS (1)

In the wilderness.

### WORDS (2)

Shall we speak?

### WORDS (3)

They will stone me.

---

### GEMATRIA 251
*for Edmond Jabes*

The desert
speaks.

---

### A MULTITUDE (1)

Their anger
for food.

### A MULTITUDE (2)

Thousands of
messengers.

---

GEMATRIA 259

In a coffin.
In the ark.

In the ark.
In the wilderness.

———————

CHERUBIM

My horse
commanded them.

———————

GEMATRIA 286

His city
& a city
& cities of
his city.

———————

EVENING (1)

For the light.

EVENING (2)

Burnt out.

EVENING (3)

In passing.

———————

**TO CLEANSE THEM:**

Standing
in the basin.

---

**GEMATRIA 288**

Buds
from the womb
had budded.

---

**A PREY (1)**

Torn in pieces.

**A PREY (2)**

Plucked.

---

**BE FRUITFUL**

with a fist!

---

**EVIL (1)**

A city.

**EVIL (2)**

Eyes of
kings.

Sodden, cooked
lambs.

IMAGINATION (1)

Surely.

IMAGINATION (2)

Vain.

IMAGINATION (3)

Empty.

DOMINION

His parable.

FINS / TEETH

A bone
they scrape off.

FLESH (1)

& its flesh-hooks.

FLESH (2)

that lusted.

FLESH (3)

Enclosed.

## TWELFTH GEMATRIA
"Imagination"

IMAGINATION (1)

A wing'd
shoe.

IMAGINATION (2)

Spices
ascending.

IMAGINATION (3)

A nest
that raised you up.

———————————

IN THE MIDST (1)

In the morning.

IN THE MIDST (2)

In the grave.

———————————

DARKNESS

& a lamb.

———————————

**TWIN GEMATRIA**

Seventy
according to their number.

Blue
according to their tongues.

---

**THOU, THEE**

& he kissed him.

---

**A PERVERSION**

She was afraid
& he woke up.

---

**GEMATRIA 404**
"A Sodomite"

My angel.
Your anger.

Your anger.
His mouth.

---

**ROUND ABOUT**

According to its borders.

---

**MYRIADS (1-3)**

To remove
a foreskin:

grass
on your feet

& the purple
lamb.

---

**SKIN HARPS**

from my flesh.

---

## EUPHRATES, EUPHRATES

Thirty
cows

grope
in the plains:

Euphrates
Euphrates.

---

## GEMATRIA 692

A scar.
A quarter.

A fortified
scar.

---

## WRITTEN

Wreathen.

---

PENETRATING STREAKS (1 & 2)

Three
lights

& three
horsemen.

---

GEMATRIA 806

(1)
Old
jars.

(2)
Doing it
roughly.

---

with lips

of linen

& crushed.

---

**EIGHT**

Eight.
Eight.

Double
eight.

---

**IN BLUE (1)**

Her breasts
were done.

**IN BLUE (2)**

Her breasts
for you.

**IN BLUE (3)**

For thee.
For thee.

---

**PHILISTINES**

& their pins.

---

GEMATRIA 906
"Scarlet"

(1)
Scarlet
shoulder pieces.

(2)
Scarlet
& scarlet.

---

RED DREAMS

Flashing up.

---

GEMATRIA 1212
"His Desire"

(1)
She saw
streaks.

(2)
Bones
& a turtledove.

(3)
Holy.
Holy.
Holy.

# MORE GEMATRIAS
## 1-100

1

His red
unclean
blood.
Earth
& water.
The adam, the man.
Fat
& bloody. [50]


2

THE ANGEL (1)

A star
shall uncover.

THE ANGEL (2)

His king. [96]


3

GEMATRIA 105

Man,
the blasphemer.

Man
the bald locust.

4

YOUR STUFF

My stuff
is unclean. [120]


5

THE PLAGUE

Hands
that begot thee. [128]


6

A WIZARD (1)              A WIZARD (2)

Between me                Let us sacrifice
& Leah.                   your son.
                                        [144]


7

EAST

Night
in your hearts. [149]

8

Benjamin,
the old man,

brought us up,
a living substance

in your sight,
like sheep

he has upheld
your flock—

out of the thousands
—& has brought

a sprig of calamus
& wormwood

money
in your eye

& birds
& from his people

in the tree
an unjust gain

they rose up,
they shall rise up					[161, 162]

9

STREAKED (1)

Great
twisted cords.

STREAKED (2)

Be white
& pipe.

STREAKED (3)

His throne
is washed.

[174]

10

THE PREY / THE REFUGE

I will go out
into the water.

[184]

11

A BONE

against you.

[202]

12

TO CURSE YOU / A CHARM
                for H.B.

(1)
Bloom
the unclean.


(2)
I will blot him out
with stones.

(3)
Sodom
in Sodom.                                                 [210]


13

THE LIGHT

will multiply.                                        [212]


14

MY WORDS
    *for Charles Olson*

To see for oneself.                              [216]

15

THE JEW (1)

A bastard.

THE JEW (2)

With guile.

[287]

16

GEMATRIA 300

A ransom
& a purple
candlestick
for sale.

The curtain
will set.

Empty, vain.

Only
balm
for your sake,

only
formed,
torn by beasts &
uncircumcised.

Imagination.

Pomegranates of
atonement.

17

GEMATRIA 308

He will bathe
with honey

perfumes

& at night
will return
bald
as an agate

his grave
near at hand.


18

RETURN! (1)

& he returned.

RETURN! (2)

& he stayed put.   [318]


19

LAST NIGHT

Guilty.                                                                                          [341]

20

MOSES (1)

The legs.

MOSES (2)

The hoofs.

MOSES (3)

A bearded
vulture. [345]

21

THE NAME (1)

The book.

THE NAME (2)

There. [345]

22

FIVE (1)

like snow.

FIVE (2)

And they asked. [353]

23

MESSIAH

A snake.

[358]

24

GEMATRIA 366

Naked
& scarlet.

•

Naked
& leprous.

•

Naked
& old.

•

His horns
drop down.

25

A NUMBER (1)

Wailing
a number.

A NUMBER (2)

Numbered
the end.

[368/380]

26

AGAINST A MAN

Those who hate him. [381]

27

WHETHER (1)

Concerning.

WHETHER (2)

On the left.

[411]

28

GEMATRIA 432

And they heard
your house

your household

the daughters of
your houses

their bodies
shameful

inside
a perversion
of the soul.

29

THE JUDGMENT (1)

In a flame.

THE JUDGMENT (2)

In your house.   [434]

30

JUDITH

The hawk
chews
her eyes.                                              [435]


31

GEMATRIA 438
"An Inscription"

To this
with its life.

And Tubal
with his soul.

And your household
with their weeping.

*The written
power is gone.*

32

GEMATRIA 444

cakes

/

& cakes

/

& a cake of


33

DEATH (1)

Let him die.

DDEATH (2)

The moon
like a stranger.

[446]

34

GEMATRIA 456
"Fear"

You will become unclean
You will become unclean

You will defile yourselves
in uncleanness

You will go
You will die

You will die
in uncleanness

*And she went*
*And he died*

*And he died*
*And it ended*


35

A BURNING

Remember
a foot.

[466]

36

GEMATRIA 461

Loops of
loops.

Have I eaten
with you?

In her banishment.
Ships.

Loops of
loops.

I have eaten
my terror.

37

GEMATRIA 469

Your fathers
& their saddles.
Our fathers
in ships.

38

GEMATRIA 482
"A Prophecy"

when they are dead,
enclosed
among you,
white
in knowledge
& in booths,
you will wash
your daughters—

according to the writings
& the later rain


39

A CARCASS

Your first-born
has blessed you.                                [484]


40

A BEAUTIFUL KNIFE

(1)
The curtain
& your eye.


(2)
Imagination
hidden.


(3)
We die
& are beautiful.                                [496]

41

GEMATRIA 499

The frogs.

•

The hosts.

I call to witness.

42

GEMATRIA 506

Her head
giving suck.

Gall,
her food.

"I have served you
an ox.

Will you eat it?"

43

GEMATRIA 507

you will eat
her flesh,
her belly

& the poison
you will spew out
will consume us

& our lands:
you will eat it
& go forth


44

GEMATRIA 508

Silence.
A night hawk.

Black
wagons.

Deaf
flesh.

45

**GEMATRIA 519**
"Around Midnight"

so he drove out
& was silent

& she took it
& when it rose

sang
the song

at their door
around midnight

46

**SUDDENLY**

Their words are
a cry.

[521]

47

**THE LANGUAGE OF THE BEES**

He was silent. [523]

48

LIKE HIS FLESH

Jordan
burning.

[528]

49

PIECES (1)

Removing
the pieces.

PIECES (2)

The vineyard
cried.

[528]

50

FLESH (1)

Show me
an image.

FLESH (2)

A pillar.

FLESH (3)

Sold
in the gutters.

[532]

51

**KINGDOMS (1)**

He was angry.

**KINGDOMS (2)**

She was despised.

**KINGDOMS (3)**

His kingdom.  [532]

52

**TWINED**

with its feathers.

[547]

53

**GEMATRIA 548**

A scab
from his flesh.

A sickle.

Trembling
at evening.

54

GEMATRIA 556

The first
worms
carry us up.

The remaining one
flies
your commandments.

55

YOUR LOINS

The thighs
he stripped naked.                                [560]

56

GEMATRIA 560

Snow.

•

The evil
shepherd.

•

And at evening
their thighs.

57

**SAD GEMATRIA**

I am old

•

•

•

& I fell down.

[567]

58

**GEMATRIA 570**

Ten
fountains.

•

A hairy
bed.

•

Straight,
void,
fruitful,
smashed.

•

Hair
like an eagle.

59

FOUNTAINS

& wonders. [576]

60

GEMATRIA 580

Serpents.

Asps.

Demons.

A fiery serpent.

61

GEMATRIA 582

flowers
torn in pieces

adornments of
the earth

62

GEMATRIA 586
"The Goat"

They blow
a horn

& burn
its dung.


63

BURNING

A light from
the river.                                                [590]


64

A SWARM (1)                         A SWARM (2)

They shall spread.                   More.
                                                         [596]

65

GEMATRIA 600

(1)
Eagles.

(2)
Eyes
kill
the light.

(3)
A fire
in his land.

(4)
See
the darkness.

(5)
Beautiful
Sodom.

(6)
Always
his eyes.

(7)
Angels of
bone
in your seed.

## 66

**TWO GEMATRIAS FOR TED ENSLIN**

*Forms* (1)

Imagination
a fire.

*Forms* (2)

The uncircumcised
rock.                                                   [601]


## 67

**GEMATRIA 610**

(1)
Her mistress
greenish.
My bones
spread wide.


(2)
A tenth.
A tithe.
A sixth.
Ten thousands.

## 68

### THE BRIGHT SPOT (1)

When he came down.

### THE BRIGHT SPOT (2)

The fire
in his skin.

### THE BRIGHT SPOT (3)

A woman like
honey.

[612]

## 69

### A COVENANT (1)

A foreskin
restored.

### A COVENANT (2)

A fake
foreskin.

[612]

## 70

### GEMATRIA 619

The spirits.
The end.

•

Plump
& fat.

71

THE LAST

[621]

like the first one.


72

TAMAR (1)

A naked
boy.

TAMAR (2)

Like the rain.

[640]

73

GEMATRIA 646

The lights
of his ribs.


74

GEMATRIA 655

The boards.
The lamps.

The turtledoves.
The demons.

And a deep sleep.

75

GEMATRIA 676

Nakedness.

Blindness.

They lay down
& he lay down.

I will hide.

76

GEMATRIA 678

As he fed
& was famished

you will kindle
& burn.

77

STRANGERS

she sent out
like spies                                             [686]

78

GEMATRIA 690

Palm trees.

Candlesticks.

Curtains.

Hoof
of a lamb.


79

GEMATRIA 693
"The Hebrew Women"

His name
at noon.

•

Her name
far off.

•

Rejoice
in the lamb.

80

GEMATRIA 700

An ark cover.
A foreskin.

A foreskin.
A veil.

You have turned aside.


81

THE SABBATH

A tooth
for a tooth.                                              [702]


82

GEMATRIA 723

You will slaughter
& I will bring back.

You will slaughter
& you will sow.

You will slaughter
& you will slaughter.

83

GEMATRIA 730

You will lend upon interest.
You are covered with fat.


84

DIVINATION (1)

Ears of corn
in the firmament.

DIVINATION (2)

Your bed
like a bed.

[764]


85

GEMATRIA 780

Heaven.
He made you.

Oil.
From my book.

In the ashes.
Heaven.

Eleven.

Alone.

86

GEMATRIA 796

The maidservant
will lie with her.

•

Trumpets.

•

Out of his sleep.

•

The maidservant.

Send me away.

87

UNDER YOUR MAID

Be dismayed.
Be dismayed. [808]

88

THANKSGIVING

Your lips. [810]

89

GEMATRIA 828

Families
& jars.

And imprints
of families.


90

PHILISTINES

Shekels
for wives.

[860]

91

GEMATRIA 870

I had followed
a coat.

92

NETWORK (1)

When you go.

NETWORK (2)

Your soul
in fury.

NETWORK (3)

I started
to write.                                    [900]


93

GEMATRIA 904

(1)
According to their generations.

(2)
After their pattern.

(3)
By way of their families.


94

THE ACCOUNTING (1)

Have you stolen
their sisters?

THE ACCOUNTING (2)

Have you stolen
their sacks?
                                              [910]

95

**IN PRAISE OF THE DEAD**

That they will crawl. [940]


96

**TENS**
    *for David Meltzer*

I prepared
the meathooks.

•

You guided
the timbrel.

•

It covered
the land.
[970]


97

**GEMATRIA** 980
"Burning"

You will burn
your wages.

•

A kid
will be burned.

•

Dead
in the entry.

98

GEMATRIA 988

I know
his dreams.

•

Stone
wombs.

•

Many
bruised testicles.

•

Almond blossoms.
Frogs.

•

And the open
door.

99

GEMATRIA 1082

a trumpet blast

/

first the thunders

/

the thunders, the voices
& the thunders


100

CHAINS (1)                        CHAINS (2)

Your six                          False
gates.                            eagles.        [1200]

# BEYOND GEMATRIA

GEMATRIA ONE

Laughter. Of their blood into his nostrils. Numbed. And the window numbed as well. We ate the children. We will eat their gods. We ate & we will eat. His desire will be ransomed. May my angel eat? He may. He will. He will heave a bone against you. A sodomite & angel. The confusion arising from two kinds—of bones? of angels? When the water rises into waters. As when the water rises into seas.

GEMATRIA TWO

Perhaps they do,
millennial & white—
a kingdom talks to me     your bread
is taken for a treasure
—even more the lice—
stars shine in his mouth
beneath his gums
a yellow angel rises, swelling
like a bat
a great star, fair as days
& beautiful as waters,
as her sweet mouth haunts
the man who sees
& knows a window,
if an angel by himself
becomes a cup,
also a little owl,
my heart condenses to an emerald,
water that our hearts are,
eyes, a basket from the sea,
the face his mouth took for a king's
& saved although the face

kept murmuring, the sea
drove globulets onto the land.
his bone against her, wailing,
a star is in your mouth,
your yellow god is sucking
like a dog


GEMATRIA THREE

when he sent a curse
against you
with his finger, you saw
a cloud in wood,
streaked dainties
in the rain the cloud
over his head was
empty, empty
was the vine,
your shoes were empty
& walking toward a flashing light
your eyes watched
the little numbers
wailing,
horses & a cloud,
a place *within* we asked
if we could find
& found a man who sat
astride a couch,
a man who flashes lights
& shakes a finger
like a blossom
numbering our days,
congealed
before it ends

## GEMATRIA FOUR

your mistress
conceived         I did it

(she said) for his seed
& for the fire

a blessing
for twenty

you have blesst
the fat

& the fat ones
their droppings are clean

like a field
& its flowers

plump
& fat

"these you will number
& those I will kill"


## GEMATRIA FIVE

The darkness
gushes against a second
darkness

blesst & scalded,
redder than the lamb the demons
bring, evil shepherds

who surround you,
turtledoves above & lamps
like stars, like lights

all over
the night sky,
glowing

as an oven fills with darkness,
the jews inside their cities
lost in sleep


## GEMATRIA SIX

when he came down
she saw him
she saw streaks & bones

she saw a turtledove
his neck
was in the fire

zohar in the morning
bright spots
in the grave

false
eagles,
chains

my holiness remembered

GEMATRIA SEVEN

after the man removed his hat, his words
were suddenly a cry
his songs a horned snake

gods rushed against his doors
with slime, a face
became a wheel

bricks framed a ladder
there were hollow stones
& hooks & jewels

his daughters pitched their clothes
into the gutters
the widows sprang for hats

at midnight     he was silent
but retained a place & watched
the pieces fall behind him

the way a star falls in his dreams


DOMESTIC GEMATRIA
"Home Movies"

Inward,
in her house,
a beast
sinned,
souls fell lusting.
You shall bring
my sister.

(Yes.)
Your wives
like wives
—like birds inside—
his house—
your daughter whom they stripped
& let her be.


A GEMATRIA FOR HORSEMEN

Three horsemen
will be cut off.

•

Three
& three.

To seek it out.
To see it.

To rejoice.

•

Three
fiery
horsemen.

•

Three
for six.

•

The horsemen.
Three.

•

I have cut a covenant
for six

& I will come down
falsely.

KHURBN GEMATRIA [266]

1

The oppression
will smite

the camp
with thirst

& dust:
the plague

is in your barns
the camp

delivered
to their gods

2

a wheel
dyed red

an apparition

set apart

out of the furnace


3

from his youth
she bound him

afterwards
they turned aside
& went

his streams
their vineyards

an apparition
that was at the end

sold
in the gutters

"show me"

"I will turn aside"

## PAPER AIRS

### A GAME OF CARDS

Pharaoh.
Faro.
Landing lights.

### DISGUST

The sky clears up,
uncramps him.

### TRANSITIONS

Ballistics.

### THE ONE-EYED MAN

takes out the stains:
malpractice!

### TIRE TREADS

Space.
Room.
Duration.
Time.

### THE DREAMER

From dictation,
pawns his heart.

### A FLOWER-HOLDER

Just like me.

### THE EXPEDITION

starts an anchor
like a trowel,
soon transplaced.

### PAPER AIRS

They beat the ground
for animals.
They round up thieves.

### THE QUESTION

Torture as
constraint. He makes himself
at home.

### AN EARLY PEAR

In my opinion.

IN THE COOL OF THE EVENING

*There is nothing for you here*
the chauffeur grumbles. *Who
has pinched my matches?*


GREMLINS

Licorice as sex.


COLD RIVETS


COLD RIVETS

Third year syllabus

•

OLD AGE

Stand by the wall.
Sit at the window.
At the scene of the crime.


ECLIPSE

A foot stands in the doorway.

**THE DAY OF REST**

A bonfire.
Howls or shrieks of joy.

**A MORAL COWARD**

He eats a cold meal in the evening.

**BLOOD CLOT**

A pebble.
Broken flint.
The art of driving.

**TORPOR**

At the point of death.

**A LITTLE MAN**

Sweat rolling off
his forehead, raining
on the priest.

**THIEVES**

With solemn manners.
Hooks set in squares.

THE WHIP

This wall obstructs the view.


LINES COMPOSED ACCORDING
TO THE LAWS OF CHANCE

A horn blows in my ears.
The whole town's talking.
When the fruit turns red.


THE DEMIGOD (1)

lies waiting,
drunk & gay,
run down by horses.


THE DEMIGOD (2)

Old gelding
founders.


PROGRESS
    *for Barrett Watten*

Apple fritters.

A HINT

Provokes to anger.
Burning.
Glowing.
Dynamite.
The golden mean.


PLURALITIES

They strip the flesh off.
Tear the clothes to shreds.


NATURAL HISTORY (1)

of ropes & cables.

NATURAL HISTORY (2)

Going downstream
like a cushion.

NATURAL HISTORY (3)

distracts me.

NATURAL HISTORY (4)

Construction of a sentence.
On a map.

**NOTHING**

A country full of woods.
An empty belly.

# 14 STATIONS

*for Arie Galles*

The full series of fourteen poems was written to accompany Arie Galles's monumental charcoal drawings derived from World War II aerial views of the principal Nazi extermination camps—each with an attendant railroad station—known even then to have been the sites of holocaust. As Galles worked from documentary photographs to establish some pretense at distance (= objectivity), I decided to objectify by turning again to gematria as a way to determine the words and phrases that would come into the poems. The counts were made off the Hebrew and/or Yiddish spelling of the camp names, then keyed to the numerical values of Hebrew words and word combinations in the first five books of the Bible. It was my hope that this small degree of objective chance would not so much mask feeling or meaning as allow it to emerge.


THE FIRST STATION: AUSCHWITZ-BIRKENAU

*now the serpent:*

I will bring back
their taskmasters
crazy & mad

will meet them
deep in the valley
& be subdued

separated in life
uncircumcised, needy
shoes stowed away

how naked they come
my fathers
my fathers

angry & trembling
the serpents
you have destroyed

their faces remembered
small in your eyes,
shut down, soiled

see a light
take shape in the pit,
someone killed

torn in pieces
a terror, a god,
go down deeper


THE SECOND STATION: BABI YAR

he was angry
& smelled
like the righteous

slew
the clean & pure,
ran over them

& they went down
before us
faint

& streaked,
the bars
along the way

increased & multiplied
before our eyes
their place

spread far & wide,
was like my spirit
& my sword

that made you see


THE THIRD STATION: BUCHENWALD

deliver me
from them

your cattle
rising

your assembly
lords of fat

deliver me
from color


THE FOURTH STATION: BELZEC

of those who had escaped,
the children foremost,
he would take some as witnesses

"leave me to drink
"among the goats
"that you may eat & I be eaten

"when life becomes a terror
"your strength against the children
"& her children blotted out


## THE FIFTH STATION: BERGEN-BELSEN

1

gates
round about me

I knew
& you know

& she had compassion
(alive)

a carcass
a carcass

& a dancing
carcass


2

& I will kill
the fat
& the fat ones

the wicked
the he-goats
your mistress

conceived
like a coat
& torn off

like the twenty
those you ran over
& numbered

& like those
I will kill


THE SIXTH STATION: GROSS-ROSEN

& naked there among
the swarming things

we saw them
in the dung

bright spots
bright spots

that she did stare at
& would see them burn


THE SEVENTH STATION: DACHAU

heart
dim
& sore

his hands
slow
& heavy

& so he looked,
his glory
weeping

## THE EIGHTH STATION: CHELMNO

1
*A Chorus of Children*

we dreamed
& he changed:
an armed man
but delicate,
driven,
someone who touches us,
touches
our thighs,
strips us naked,
to wound us,
a fugitive,
evil,
aggrieved,
who punishes,
slays us
at evening

2
*A Chorus of Survivors*

the word
that you feared
like hail
on the mountain
& feared
what would cause it to shine,
to be seen,
like her belly,
like hooks,
like the wheat
on our altars,
all will be eaten,
will not be
a sacrifice
there with the nations,
but a curse
in her womb


THE NINTH STATION: TREBLINKA

the voices, thunders
& the voices
of our kin
that they will bring in
from the top

the kingdoms gathering
to kill us
& you will wave
o Israel
& will submit yourself

& I will set apart
the sum of them
the thunders, voices
& the thunders
I will watch & will take heed


## THE TENTH STATION: MAUTHAUSEN

your camp
brings me
the war
that bore you,

made you inherit
the plague,
your children
torn from you,

your hands that spawned
the offspring of
the nations,
a stone against them

from my hand,
my hand against them
& a plague
between us

## THE ELEVENTH STATION: MAIDANEK

1

a thing
spoken
speaks in me

I see
the spoken
thing

a word
hail
pestilence

& from your face
a curse
is poured out

& a bone
is set in motion
spoken

in disgust
to see
the one who speaks it


2

a foreigner,
you say,
the dew like blood

her city
broken
empty for her sake

has blessed you,
seed of them
I will pursue

& you will say
in blood:
leave me alone


**THE TWELFTH STATION: SOBIBOR**

1
as he had spoken
from the wilderness:
be fruitful!

(& they were fruitful)

so he could blind them
with a fist
& cut them —

& she could take from them
the vision of
his cities

2
a skin
harp
& a boil

according to its words

how blind
& evil
like its skin

your words
erased


## THE THIRTEENTH STATION: RAVENSBRUCK

1
in my name she placed
an offering of dust

an offering of graves
where she lay empty

desolate, lay guilty
for her pleasures

in my name, the lamb
approaching

placed the basin
at her neck

throughout your generations

2
*For Rachel, twice:*

she turned aside,
I thought,
the wood, the thorns
wounding my thighs

& when they came
& carried her away
he gave them numbers
by the sword

a bell
for those with numbers


**THE FOURTEENTH STATION: STUTTHOF**

the evil water
in my dream

has emptied out
their cities

like my mouth
a hole

& in the blood
they burn

they turn them
into smoke

## POST/FACE

Gematria—a form of traditional Jewish numerology—plays off the fact that every letter of the Hebrew alphabet is also a number, & that words or phrases the sums of whose letters are equal are at some level meaningfully connected. In the course of compiling *A Big Jewish Book*, I came across a number of traditional combinations of words associated (usually in pairs) through gematria, & I juxtaposed one of the words with the other so as to form miniature poems. A few years later I came across Gutman G. Locks's *The Spice of Torah—Gematria*, which offers easy access to the numerical value of every word in the first five books of the Hebrew Bible. With its more than three hundred pages of Hebrew word lists translated into English words & phrases, I began to construct new poems based on combinations that I discovered or that I calculated on my own. Unlike the traditionalists of gematria, I have seen these coincidences / synchronicities not as hermeneutic substantiations for religious & ethical doctrines, but as an entry into the kinds of correspondences / constellations that have been central to modernist & "post"modernist poetry experiments over the last century & a half.

I have proceeded in these works in several different ways: by using one word or word-phrase as title & others (numerically equivalent) as poem; by using the gematria number as a title & constructing poems of single lines &/or stanzas of two or several lines that fall under or add up to that number; & in the section titled "Beyond Gematria," by using a freer selection of words brought to my attention by gematria, but combining & adding to them with considerably more freedom of choice. (While the last two series in "Beyond Gematria"—"Paper Airs" & "Cold Rivets"—are not gematrias as such, they seem to me to be related both in language & intention.) Several gematria poems are dedicated to contemporary & predecessor poets, because they involve words that have some connection to poems written or poetics practiced by those poets. In the final sequence, "14 Stations," gematria has served me as a form of *distancing* that brought me *closer*, paradoxically, to the supercharged & vital subject of the Jewish holocaust.

To the degree that all such works are substantially aleatory, they are full of surprises that have added greatly to my own excitement in the act of writing. At any rate I feel that the process used, in this case at least, is not irrelevant to a reading of the resulting poems.

JEROME ROTHENBERG
Encinitas, California
2009

www.ingramcontent.com/pod-product-compliance
Lightning Source LLC
LaVergne TN
LVHW011420080426
835512LV00005B/167